# TURNING

# Adam Horovitz

# TURNING

HEADLAND

First published in 2011
by
HEADLAND PUBLICATIONS
38 York Avenue
West Kirby, Wirral
CH48 3JF

British Library Cataloguing in Publication Data.
A full CIP record for this book is available from the British Library
ISBN
978 1 902096 10 0

HEADLAND acknowledges the financial
assistance of Arts Council England

Printed in Great Britain by
Oriel Studios, Orrell Mount
Hawthorne Road, Merseyside L20 6NS

for Anne

# ACKNOWLEDGEMENTS

I would like to thank the editors of *Tears in the Fence, New Departures, Hand + Star* and *Tellus*, in which some of these poems have appeared.

'Wall' and a version of 'A House Built from Cloth' appeared in *Another Way Home* (PhotoStroud, 2009). A version of 'Burials' appeared in *Oral* (Sceptre, 1999). 'Dandelion Clock' originally appeared on *Asking a Shadow to Dance* (Oxfam DVD, 2009). 'The Memory of Water' originally appeared in *Soul of the Earth* (Awen, 2010). 'Woldgate Woods' originally appeared in *The Listening Shell* (Headland, 2010). 'The Welcoming Party' originally appeared in *Adrian: Scotland Celebrates Adrian Mitchell* (Markings, 2009).

'Training Run' was commissioned by Carol Ann Duffy as part of a selection of sports poems for *The Guardian* and appeared in the paper in June 2010. 'Clearances', 'Vanishment' and 'Prelude' were written as part of a commissioned response to Emily Smith's Darbyshire prize-winning exhibition, *Retrace: Scripting Memory*, in 2009. 'On the Broken Road' was originally commissioned as a response to an artwork by the Spanish artist Jaume Prohens for an exhibition of art and poetry at the Illustration Gallery, Stroud in 2007. The quotation in 'The Root of a Scream' is from Frances Horovitz's 'Letter to My Son', which appears in *Collected Poems* (Bloodaxe, 1985).

I would like to acknowledge the help and encouragement of a great many people, including the late Inge Laird, Richard Vick, Jon Andriessen, Jo Bell, Philip Rush, Anne Stevenson, Amy Perry, Bob Thornycroft, Lucy Trevitt, Graham Smith and Susan Stephenson. I am indebted to Liz Loxley, Calum Kerr and Wendy Smith Meyer for critiques of 'The Great Unlearning' and to Adam Donen for arguing with me about 'The Death of Icarus' so enthusiastically that I wrote the Daedalus poems in response. I must particularly thank Anne Garcin for the use of her extraordinary stained glass on the cover, and Carol Ann Duffy and Gillian Clarke for their support and encouragement.

# CONTENTS

## Fugue

And always it comes back to this
once school is shut away:
a badger in my room,
its raw earth and sawdust stench
on my tongue,
needle fur salting
and souring my cheek.

And beneath the fur
the press of tarmac,
skin scarred, dented
by a hard fist of car,
the subtle musk
of an unclenched boot
warm as a womb.

And in my room,
the careful shadow of a taxidermist
stalking pools of cloth,
upturned boats of words,
glass eyes skittering in his hand like coins,
the driver's grief like a pillar of rain,
a knock of daylight on the window.

Elsewhere, the wet earth turned,
the pile diminishing,
the sett like an unfilled grave.
And in my arms, the badger –
held back from its river crossing
till I load it with fury
to carry off into the dark.

# A House Built From Cloth

I grew up in a house built from cloth
played in the ruins of cottage industry
old stones like teazle teeth
chewing at my feet

fragments of industry
their lime-wash white
faded to a smoker's gold.

I grew up in a valley
stretched over stone like cloth
rolled footballs and roller-skates
over sheep-felted grass

built locks
in the stream
under the old trade road.

I grew up in a landscape
where hedges and dry stone walls
ran through the fields like seams
where the past

was a runic language
stitched, dyed and woven
into oracular hills.

Time settles like ordered cloth
in these valleys
catches itself red handed
as it is folded back.

I grew up watching the past
pulling the weight of the future
along the canal's linear thread.

## Cheese Kisses

In a bright kitchen the colour of custard
the black cat's curling out of a yawn
on the long pine table
spread for the beginnings of a meal.

The oven is hot and creaking.
My mother turns to it, dons her striped blue and grey apron.
Hair hides her face as she bends to check the baking,
all but her eyes, which laugh at me.

A knock at the door. *Come in,* she calls.
Bill swings in smiling
the muck of gardens on his boots
She turns, rests against the cooker, greets him warmly.

*He still away?* asks Bill. A nod, hair bobbing, and a smile.
I watch in silence as the game begins.
Too young to call it flirting,
all I know is that I've been sidelined.

I watch, jealous, tease the cat.
There is fire suddenly – her apron strings
have caught on the hob.
My mother's backside is on fire.

Bill swings her round, slaps.
The fire goes out. There is silence in the kitchen
but for my laughter, asking for the trick
to be worked again.

Bill leaves quickly.
Out of the oven
come cheese kisses, which melt
in my mouth only.

## Clearances

*for Anne*

The boxes I am shifting
and sifting through
exhale as I open them,
pour out cards, photographs,
letters I have long thought lost.
The past is tracing itself on my fingers,
spreading and staining
like cigarette tar.

My mother is here.
I see her flickering,
bleached as old film,
a sepia ghost of the technicolour past.
She is caught in litanies of dust
winding up through my narrow attic
on beams of low-slung winter light
projected through a screen of velux glass.

She is delicate as snakeskin,
a rough slip of memory
formed from powdered cobwebs
the fragile pulp of quick-grown trees
and steady curlicues of ink.
A cloud crosses the sun.
As suddenly as she has come
she is gone.

You find me tear-stained, transfixed
in sunlight, a birthday card
inscribed 'To my dearest son
with love on his 7th birthday'
clasped in my hand,
its faded primroses creased.
You reach
into the nearly empty box.

## The Blackbird

*i.m. Anthony Hodge*

This morning, a blackbird swooped
into the heart of my garden
as I stood at the window
bleary as an April cloud,
a dressing gown hanging
from the dry stone wall of my waking
like a cowl of ivy.

It cocked its head
as if listening for the dreams
of cats stalking the sofa's edge,
one button eye alert to my silence,
then shifted its feet
like a cheerful drunk come home too late
and sang you into being.

All day I've seen its song of you
dancing in hedgerows,
at the pavement's edge,
clutching Herb Robert like a wine glass
reaching for the sun.
A shivering flute-memory
in the green of spring.

## Burials

I remember you telling me
of a burial years ago in Elcombe woods
up at the high point, the stony point
where local workmen
chewing their cud of cider
refused to work.
They told the husband that his wife
would get no further down
than three feet, you said,
although the grave was eventually dug.

You seemed astonished,
questioned the sanctity of such an act
siding in Protestant horror
with the old rogues buried in their pints
who mix and match their myths to suit the night.
You closed off when I told you I had dug the grave
with the family of the deceased two years before,
had stood, at six foot four, shoulder deep
in consecrated earth,
carving out a fragment of the hill.

It was as if I disappointed you,
gave you a truth you did not need
intruding on your tale with pick and spade.
All stories tell truths. I know that now.
Unwritten memories and bodies
subside like pit villages
but they leave small spaces
where poppies and dandelions grow
amongst resurgent grass.
All burials are beginnings.

## Wall

*"With chiselled touch*
*The stone unhewn and cold*
*Becomes a living mould."*
        *from a sonnet by Michelangelo Buonarroti (1475–1564)*

It is more animal now than wall.
Built in a summer a year ago
it has asserted permanence
by taking for a spine
the mismatched trees lining the road.

Depending on the season
it wears a coat of lilac,
elderflower, Old Man's Beard or just
a fine jacket of ochre leaves.
A serrated smile of stone

this wall snaps landscape into sharp relief
each jagged tooth a totem
describing the past that shaped it:
billions of crushed shells; a biography in stone,
punctuated in sweat from the builder's hands.

## Training Run

*for Ashley Loveridge*

Linear. Beyond lines. Path swallowed
by the mare's tail flick of cow parsley.
Your feet pound out the hollowed
laughter of this discarded canal. A sparse lee

in the woods jolts you awake,
out of the hammered dream of the run;
it writhes with the scent of rain, aches
under a blanket of wild garlic, sun.

You have bitten, sharp as an arrow,
into the low heat of the dusk,
the deep focus, the valley's marrow.
The world is a husk

until you run it, until you find your way
over nettle creep, cow dung, hard-trodden clay.

## On the Broken Road

a goat stutters like an ice-choked engine
   in the slow dark of morning
wheels crunch out awkward rhythms
   feet slap on fists of stone

escape is a task for many shoulders
   and ribs crack to the tick of a clock
the air is heavy with ammonia
   eyes open like refrigerators

we carry the world in a handcart
   until it can bear to carry us

## Spring Fragment

A break in the cloud,
spring come early.

The grass is rising,
a pale green tide.

I wake to a mayhem
of sharpened birdsong

blue tits scuffling in the trees
like buzz-bomb winos.

They dart along a spine
of red brick

a chittering wall of echoes
a dust of feathers.

In their tiny puddles of shadow
cats recoil like guns.

## Shells

A lead sky and your belly
taut beneath my fingers

the tender mouths of cows
rustling the grass.

Water slips uneasily through pipes
into a worn stone trough.

Your mouth is an egg split by our tongues,
passion hatching in the quiet dark of rain.

Mud sucks at our feet,
whitethorn blossom consumes us.

Expecting discovery, we cling
to the hard nugget of warmth

beneath our skins, the cocoon of lust
waiting for urgent sun, brilliant wings.

Home is a broken shell, an act of imagination
lost in the long grass, in newly budded leaves.

## After the Party

I bought myself time to become
human under the covers

subsumed in your scent,
last night's wine

arch on my tongue, allowed
myself hours for flesh to fill out

rolling through the bed's
curved memory of you.

And you? You rose like a falcon
making a pinpoint of its shadow

high above the bruised earth,
sunlight feathering your hair.

You swept the sky of stars
on your way to work

hangover running beneath you
like an escaping hare.

## Dandelion Clock

Starch-tongued morning,
the pub floating like brassy nirvana
in the ache of memory.
A dressing gown wraps the day in soil and grass.

Beetles crawl from the shower head
eager to escape the bathroom,
find a blazing ball of dung
to roll up into the sky.

I stretch like a wind-racked tree,
the marrow creaking in my bones.
Outside, someone has thrown
a toilet roll across the sky.

Body dressed, eyes unbuttoned,
paracetamol leaping in my blood
like unboxed Jack, I slam through the door
and drift away into beds of flowers.

Hellebore skulk by the wall waiting,
hangdog as hunted royalty, for their last cigarette.
Butter-naveled primroses simper in clusters
bobbing their heads above green newspaper leaves.

White stars I cannot name blaze on mossy stone.
St David's heralds stoop into April
One dandelion clock remains from yesterday,
fragile and un-ticked.

   I regard it cautiously
      not sure yet
  whose head
    will dissipate first...

## The Memory of Water

It was life to us, the rain
in the cold days of upheaval before the fall;
it was mouse patterings on a ceiling of leaves,
a sweet dishevelling
carrying the scent of change.
Like the swallows it came, back
and back again to the places it remembered.

This dust-wheel plain was forest once.
Deep underneath, where nuts and seeds snuggle in,
their ability to grow suspended by the drought,
the memory of water echoes
in empty caverns that were lakes,
shivers in parched fibres, patient as a spider.

Sometimes the rain came down
in a ritual showering, a breathy song of cloud.
Or, in the boomy slate-grey mornings
it was the rush of trains.
We marked the days with it, the seasons
as it balanced on the edge of the horizon
like a scavenging gull.
We were never sure whether we wanted it
to break on our heads like dark, ripe apples
although we loved it when it came.

But the rain that clung like silk,
that slithered in through clothes
to the moist valleys of the flesh,
that is the rain I remember.
The rain that sweetened the breath of gardens,
that clung to your breast like a kiss.
That is the rain I will take with me to my dying.
Let me show you, with my lips,
exactly how it felt.

## Summer Storm

I am curled like a cat
oblivious to post and news
in the slack mouth of the house.

Rain echoes in the watering can
like the ghost of an old school bell,
falls as scattered applause on the lawn.
I am submerged
in absence fragrant as leaf mould.

You have taken your raven drawings
and flown before dawn. The world is quiet
but for the hiss
of tree and water.
There is nothing beyond this garden

but you. The cars have all choked on
tongues of wet tarmac,
the lines of power, of communication, have fizzled out.
I am faced with silence,
the word in seed form.

My head is hard as a poppy pod
and the sky is dark.
You have taken your drawings
of thought and memory
to carve into the god's head at Trondheim,

the blessing place of kings
and all I can do is curl like a cat and listen
to the thunder whispering your name.

## Love Poem

This is a town of glass, of lenses.
We walk through
      hand in hand,
the mirror-language of love
on the buds of our tongues,
ghosting in the corners of our eyes.

Wars are prickly,
pale as lavender; we pass them by,
step over politics, duck all news.
Honeymooning in a greenhouse,
the sun is our only guest
except for the television,
silenced with a finger
      by our lips.

We do not step outside
to ogle our reflections,
just bed down in this glass bulb,
this town we have un-peopled
as we stir the salad
with a spoon of blood.

## Woldgate Woods

*in response to the painting by David Hockney*

Moss and leaf shrivelling underfoot,
trees like brainstems thinking out the sky.
Follow a pen-scribble of undergrowth
(hunger scribed in the teeth of bramble, foxes)

through breaks of faded grass (sun clearings
where midges punctuate a parchment of dusk)
then back into the abbey of shadow,
the cluttered unsilence of prayer and fear

where gods stand rooted or lie blotted,
(crumbling into iambic, fungal paths
for ants and earwigs) and badgers lurch
after sacrifices of root or flesh.

The wood holds secrets in parenthesis
(sly qualifying trees like wombs of verse).

## Walking in Normandy

I walked for two hours under woods
cool as snowfall, filled with the encroaching
rustle of unseen hoof and tusk

and then the road bent out
into a valley blistered by daylight.
My legs dragged, swollen in the sudden heat.

Resting at a bridged-over ford, I watched
an otter flick past, its body
bullet smooth under the water's skin.

It glanced through shafts of refractory light,
air bubbles burst above it –
a sound poem of rising breath.

In the distance, tractors crooned under the weight
of sun-gorged sky. Even insects slowed
their lazy dancing along the stream's lip.

Leaning awkwardly on the bridge, I wished
that I might again be held in the river's crooked arm
transfixed, a bright otter at the edge of sight

until cars passed, clattering like distant geese
through a balloon of dust. I rose, started the slow
stump home, apple brandy caught in my nostrils.

Back to campfire and community,
to the swell of tents, the maelstrom
of children up past bedtime

all slipping crazily through the fire's fluctuating ambit,
their youth as luminescent and as brief
as bubbles in the night's stream.

## White Bone

White bone found in the scraped grass
stark as a band of cloud.
White bone found on the hip-curl crawl
up away from the sea.

White bone carried like a totem
away from the jawbone of the field.
White bone lodged in a cold pot
steep and callous as a knife.

White bone in the break
of the lime-washed wall, colder than the sea.
White bone searing the still room
heartless as a gull's screech.

White bone in your white hand
seeking out the folded reds of flesh.

## Queen Hecuba's Prayer

If my voice cracks
it is not because I am weak.

If I witness horror
I shall not become meek.

If I start at shadows
it is not because I am scared.

If my sons are broken
their pyres will be prepared.

If I say little
it is not for want of words.

If I lose my faith
feed me to the birds.

## My Invisible Aunt

An aunt I've never seen in the flesh
lurks in my grandmother's kitchen
perhaps communing with the kosher sausages.
She is avoiding me.

I had always suspected her of not existing
despite glimpsing photographs
of her with my vanished Rabbi uncle,
whose existence I also had to take on trust.

The sight of her half-remembered face
repeated like a smudged photocopy
in inquisitive men who said they were her sons
eventually proved her to be real,

but that was long ago and tonight I am
being moved like a chess piece
from room to room in an effort to preserve
the kosher space around my invisible aunt.

My grandmother smiles mournfully,
divides herself between the ghettos
my unseen aunt creates.
"She is very orthodox," my grandmother explains.

I smile politely and wonder if,
thanks to this careful separation,
my invisible aunt envisages me
as half-Jew meat or watered milk

or just as unclean animal, as pig.
I am tempted to burst through the curtains
and confront her - but she's far from being a vicar
and the noises off in this sorry farce

are those of bigotry run riot,
of prayer and weakness,
and of the foundations of her god's house
shifting in the sand she built them on.

## The Death of Icarus

We watched him fall
saw the great gold coin of sun
tip him from the sky, heard the hiss of wax on water.

He had been perfect
an alabaster god among men
and we loved his daring

watching him pirouette on heady air
our hands at our brows, masking the light.
But we also watched, dispassionate,

when he plummeted like a broken pigeon
into the sea's maw.
His death was swift and silent

and when his body
washed up on the beach
we studied his broken neck

snapped like driftwood;
the rime of salt souring
his bloodless lips.

We watched gulls pick out
the pearls of his eyes
with a jeweller's steady care

his dead legs dancing
in jerky rhythms
to the tune of the tide.

Then we plucked
those feathers that remained
to fill our pillows

covered him in sand
and walked back slowly
to our ploughs

waiting in eager silence
for the next man who would be god
to fly and fall, fly and fall.

## Crow Light

They held the space between words, the crows
in the cold corner of the field
where leaves arched from trees,
a sullen, fading rainbow.
Coarse as a mason's hand
they croaked the night into being,
their song a caustic hymn
of mildew, longing, dampened fear.
I stood in sycamore shadow
unable to move beyond the dancing mask of leaves.
Dusk built in me like smoke
as they tore the day to shreds.
I do not know if I cried out for the moon
or murdered the sun with the tongue of a crow.

## Vanishment

power lines written
on my face

through glass
warm as illuminated whisky

birds pocked in shadow-Braille
on my cheek


work is a series
of border disputes

terse exchanges
telephone ambushings

I am outflanked by email
outgunned


I am disappearing
inch by inch with the sun's set

slipping behind hills
brittle as scrubbed parchment

overwritten by the rigours
of merely getting by


all that is left of me
come dark

is the shadow
of power lines

a bleached arpeggio of bird song
a thin-lipped yawn of sun

## Jack vs. the Beanstalk

At the bottom of the beanstalk,
I shuffle papers I cannot read
and switch off birdsong with a remote control.

Four white lines become a cell;
I curse the chalk for lacking a blackboard,
the air for failing to design a door.

My mother sends letters sometimes.
She says she has climbed the beanstalk,
that she is marrying someone high up.

She sends presents with notes attached –
glib aphorisms like *You make your own luck
(but these might help).*

Bitterness stamps its passport on my face
like a nettle rash. I cannot play the harp
and the goose eggs are always overdone.

# January Haiku

No spade can dig this
earth. Winter protects itself
from all shoots of change.

\*\*

Glassy fists of frost
clasp green daffodil throats,
un-spring their breathing.

\*\*

Flat stone sun skipping
over ice, burning my eyes.
Winter phosphorous.

\*\*

The hellebore bends
like Atlas, its face purple
with the weight of frost.

\*\*

An army of ice.
Its endless, stifling shroud creeps
throughout the garden.

## Double Exposure

Trees crawl to her eyes.
Black mountains ride
her cheekbones, bracken-ridged.
The buzzard's cry
is a sheen of tears
stilled by silver nitrate.

It seems deliberate,
an alchemical trick
the photographer crafted;
paper turned to thought and memory.
The camera, a one-eyed god,
sees more than surfaces.

The face of my mother
is subsumed by a fluid world
of beasts and wilderness,
a silence that was never still.
She has become a landscape
I can hold, a fulcrum

for the weight of loss.
Time bends like winter trees
and I am eight again,
the undeveloped past
shimmering in my hands,
doubly exposed to light.

## Her Bedroom

Walls, dirty white as a seagull's wing.
One small window like an eye
purple-flecked with foxgloves
from the high hedgerows
lining the road to school.

Sunlight stops at the windowsill;
this room is a fist of twilight,
smells of the dark earth.
Shadows move through it
like earthworms.

All is whispers here:
the dresses in the wardrobe, restless,
our small, tense voices,
the fractured spider's web in the corner,
even the nearby field of lambs.

It is jewellery that marks this room:
the Celtic cross hanging from the bedpost
on a leather strap – silver scored
with lines of tarnish
black as the toad-creak floorboards –

the necklace of amber beads
coiling from a wicker basket,
source obscured,
like a stream trickling down a steep mountain
away towards the sea.

## Last Night She Saw Badgers

He stands at the school gate
hunched and trembling
like a tree at winter's rise.

The air is glue. I wade to him, each step
taking all of my twelve years.
He is grey as the rope we found in Orkney,

coiled and faded on the cliffs of Ronaldsay,
worn out with hoping for the rescue
that would never come.

The car is waiting.
*We must go to London now,* he says.
Death waits in the car, unspeaking.

I too am silent. The blood rushing
in my ears like howling trees
is noise enough for me.

I do not grasp the journey.
It is over in moments.
I am contracting time to reach my mother

in her sad bed in the stale ward
where my two plastic Star Wars toys
stand against the coming dark.

Too long I have waited in the deathly quiet
of the Vicar's house, unspeaking, ungrateful,
mapping out how I will run away to London.

Too long without news and contact,
the dreams I'd shared with her as a child
rising again like tides too urgent

for the moon to pull them back.
*Last night she saw badgers,* he tells me
as we walk into the hospital.

I remember walking with her to see a badger's sett
on the other side of the valley, the orderly piles of dung,
the cowslips, the dusk.

*Last night she saw badgers at the end of her bed.*

## The Root of a Scream

I saw
nerves severed under a laser's scrutiny
and a face collapse
eyes floating in pools of silence
breath fluttering out on phosphorous wings

I saw
pliant flesh turn to marble, colder and colder to the touch
flecked with tears and gathering dust
a lost letter: "...*if you were sitting by this bed/which I do not wish...*"
men and women hobbling with loss
grappling with words they'd rather leave unsaid

I saw
food dripping into an uninterested ocean
moulding scant colour onto the stagnant surface
before swirling irradiated into the brain's maw
while Morphine angels sang of sleep

I saw
breasts filled with chemicals
withered and feeble under my fingers
a hand clasping my wrist
*You and he are the only men who'll ever touch them again*

I saw
a clock stuck at eleven
and a man vainly pleading for life
a computer screen numbing the inevitable
the blip, blip, blip of a game
stamping on the cold root of a scream

## Turning

A high-backed chair, rocking.
Empty of you, it shifts
like a boat cutting across the river's flow.
Two coins print in my palms.

The stillness of the room is asphyxiating.
My bare feet are sore
from the carpet's hard ridges.
I reel in yew light.

The filtered sun blinks and stutters
on the spines of books.
Joyce dances with Yeats,
Bomb Culture and Jew Süss with Eliot and Pound.

The mantelpiece shivers over a sneering lip of stone.
The room is condensing around me.
Worn orange curtains stretch like curdled flame
towards the rocking chair where you are not.

Nothing is in the right place.
A vase, yellow as varnished daffodils
is here and not here, shifting between years.
A dark landscape by your would-be lover

skulks in the stair-cupboard. Only the ghostly teazles
and the flowers you painted as a girl remain constant.
I can smell pastry baking in the kitchen eight years ago
as the bone-pale chair rocks on

and I am turning in a vortex of dust,
a waxed spiral of stone and sun.
All I can hear are the yesterdays
that will not come again

in the tabby's cautious mew,
the typewriter bird's relentless, ratcheting call to arms.

The past is a sad rocking. An overlaying.
You are here and not here.

My father calls from the path;
    even his voice
 cannot hold me in one place
  as I begin to fall.

## Daedalus Laments

It was nothing but bickering
in the prison we built ourselves.
Reason was lost in the labyrinth.
We slept on cushions of boredom,

whiled away the lichen hours
in helpless dreaming. Icarus spent too much time
seeming busy as he abstracted
the feathers I'd saved to forge our passage out.

I worked. I worked, and all he learned
was endless variations on the theme of *No!*,
not preparations for our eventual escape.
I was cased in a scribbled husk

of absence, darkness. I longed for the sun,
for all I'd lost; fell into a maze of work
tied down by obsession, sublimation.
Sometimes I would look up from my desk

unsure if it was bull or boy
pawing and shivering in the clammy dark.

## The Great Unlearning

*from experience to innocence, for my father*

*i*

This age and sourness bewilders.
Where did it come from, the closeness,
the urge to hurt?
What umbilical cord binds us,
what cancer courses
through our emailed wars?
The younger I become, the less sure I am
and, now your computer has been taken away,
you are phoning in demands
for the help I have not given
because my girlfriend, who has left me
in a fit of joy, has taken all my time.

I start to work less because I am un-remembering,
disgorging books and CDs back into shops
where they wait to be unmade.
Poems are rising back into my pen.
I am lonely now; our communication a necessity
despite this inexplicable, unhealed wound in my head
that every time leads to screaming,
the storms before the calm.
You are filling out, un-wrinkling,
wiping on a beard with a drying razor.
I watch it later, shrinking into your chin
as I try to iron creases back into my clothes.

Hurt swells like a flood before the rain's rise
as we stumble the natural path towards childhood,
watching your siblings unbend,
your mother's hip heal
as she leaps from the floor of Leeside Crescent.
We try sharing a house between bouts of University.
It gets easier as I become less self-reliant,
more naïve, start shedding friends
to hide in a wounded valley
where a stone house
has pulled itself together over years to meet our needs.
Now school is coming. The great unlearning.

I get to know less about people
and stop smoking. It is a relief.
But the pain increases
and we don't know how to stop it.
We walk into the office
of a child psychologist
who tangles up our thoughts
until they resemble knots of wood.
Now, as stupid arguments about cucumbers
become mere lunch, I find myself
standing tall after a fortnight in hospital
learning how not to walk.

ii

I am much less tall than I used to be.
My shoulders hunch like walnuts,
my head is low,
the bright flush of youth at odds
with years of un-sourced grief.
And now I am packing my bags, heading for Herefordshire.
A woman I meet at the bus stop
yells at me about ingratitude
and takes me to her house
where another man claims me as his son.
Although it is all too strange for words,
it does not feel wrong.

Your late night phone calls
release me to his care
but still hurt leers
inside me like a gargoyle
and none of us can explain it or let it go.
We are too wounded
by things unimagined, unexplained.
The new man and his partner
have another child in the house.
Our mutual dislike wavers,
softens into wary hope
until he leaves with his mother for Bristol,

where I will not know them.
I am moved to a smaller house
where the smell of sweat and sorrow
rises like a molehill in the master bedroom,
am taken to a place
where poems are unsaid, harps packed away
and the bright, hard light
of tearing down appearances
hardens into tears
as we leave for a churchyard.
There, all the people we have ever known
refill the ducts in their eyes and sigh.

They are younger than I remember them;
years of sorrow lie
like clods of earth on their shoulders.
I see you there with the woman
you have been with for years
who I am only now beginning not to love.
Then a box bursts from the ground,
showering earth in an orderly pile
at the side of a deep hole.
It is carried away
on the shoulders of six men
to a place of alchemy and miracles.

Joy builds in me over several weeks,
brick by painful brick,
until I am taken to London to meet my mother.
In her hospital bed, she wakes.
Delirium becomes pain. She cries out
as they siphon morphine from her.
You are with me again, taking me to movies.
You dance and sing,
play the fool deliciously;
we become joyous in each other's company,
feeling our way to unconditional love
now my mother is alive.

There is a tender divorce in my mother's bedroom.
Two friends, like flowers waiting for the hedgerow,
stand witness by the small, dark window,
as she and the man who was my stepfather
unbind into the freedom of each other.
We move to Sunderland,
where I unlearn the hard ways of the city,
shrug off the coalface, the politics of hardship
and become innocent.
But still there is pain.
Over four years,
my mother falls slowly out of love.

iii

At first, she takes to answering your
late night calls about the leaking pipes
that healed themselves as the snows rose;
the weary burden of their absence becomes joy.
I am content to be where she is,
revelling in the newness of her,
in the selfishness of youth. I see you rarely,
contemplating the distances between us
only on empty four hour journeys
upcountry from Kings Cross.
But the need for you throbs
in my mother's ear, her blood, her womb.

Then tuneless dustmen
bring us plastic bags;
the evidence of your devotion is disgorged.
Sunderland unpicks itself, is packed in boxes.
All the time I am reducing,
my red hair becoming golden.
There is a white cloud of hope in me.
Time is expanding to encompass it.
The days are endless.
I am coming back to you,
all pain forgotten
as you leave London and its women

return to the quiet, glacier-cut valley,
the stone house we hid in,
shouting, years ago.
It is paradise.
The stream sings
of the sea it is leaving
as we play in it;
I lose all trace of troll
under the old stone bridge
you spring across goatishly.
My mother un-names the flowers,
plants sheep skulls in garlic groves.

They gather a bramble of bone,
muscle, skin and wool over the winter,
bleat back into life
as leaves dance up,
greening, to the trees.
We dance too, ecstatic in her wake,
pour cheese and onion crisps
secretly into their bags
and seal them, laugh as the cat
who walked out of the fire years ago
absorbs its kittens in your attic,
unmesses your papers.

Only one doubt remains.
How will you bear it
when, all too soon,
I am gone?

# The Welcoming Party

*i.m. Adrian Mitchell*

Beyond the lychgate,
the expected churchyard is instead a garden
tumultuous and pungent with colour;
apple trees mingling with cherries,
a snowstorm of blossom, flowers.

All the seasons are hopping together.
Roses jive with sorrel,
blushing young primroses take up
proffered palm fronds and dance amongst the clouds.
White trumpets of convolvulus blurt themselves blue.

The poets and musicians are all here:
Ginsberg jams on his harmonium
with Lennon, Lead Belly and Tom Paine;
Stevie Smith is waving from the lily pond;
Ted Hughes looms like a cliff in the distance.

Just inside the gate
William and Catherine Blake wait naked
in wicker chairs, surrounded by the flesh made word.
Blake stands, extends a hand in welcome
as the sun bursts from a page of memory

sings snatches of freedom with the voice of Lady Day.

## What Daedalus Saw

A long sleep that smelled of death;
that's all we had in the cave-dark,
in the sealed-up maze.

Voices called to us through tubes;
a torment of fragments
and a few sweet whispers that melted

into the dank of dream.
Then the light came,
the wings to the world

and we went up into the sun;
the pieces of our lives remade
in rivulets of wax.

## Prelude

Spine binary before sleeping,
fingers slipping out
dot dash melodies.

Automated music hall
of flesh on flesh,
decoding the silent day.

Bone and muscle Braille
as moon fades behind curtain
into the lower pitches.

Backache blues,
crepuscular ballads
in the soft places.

Sweat songs and spirituals,
mouth arched on neck.
The mnemonics of love.

Bed is a clean slate
overwritten in urgent wrinkles.
A prelude to dream.

## Orpheus in the Download Underworld

We make our disappearances day by day,
absence speaking for absence
through a waxed veil of leaf and seed-pod.
Territories are marked with a wing beat,
the bounds of tenderness negotiated in magpie semaphore
as we are subsumed by books,
magazines, downloads, DVDs,
gewgaws, gizmos, all those pretty
fig leaves bought to cover shame.

The house is hollow,
an echoing cave of certainties lost,
where Persephone picks pomegranate seeds
that catch in her teeth, spits them out and curses.
Cats howl around her like furies
after mice, scraps of paper,
the dust born of silence,
screwed into fists of guilt.
The goddess cries for us to stay indoors.

There is majesty in certainty if you can stomach it
but I prefer the random melt of stars,
waiting in the darkness for trees to bud,
listening for the metallic scrape of growth
as foxes slice the winter with their tongues
and owls stamp prints of mice on frosty turf.
I am walking the path away from home,
a love song balled foetal in my hand.
Follow me. I'll not look back.

Adam Horovitz has served a long apprenticeship in poetry. He has funded this by working as a barman, sheep dipper, journalist, editor and ghost writer. He has read at pubs, clubs, arts centres and festivals, including the 1996 Days of Poetry and Wine Festival in Slovenia, Glastonbury Festival and the Swindon and Cheltenham Festivals of Literature. He was poet in residence for Glastonbury Festival website in 2009 and, in 2010, was voted onto the Hospital Club and Independent newspaper's 'Hospital Club 100' as an emerging talent.

*

*Gillian Clarke* comments: 'Adam Horovitz comes of age as a poet with these vivid poems of love and loss, joy and grief, place and memory. This is his first full collection after a long apprenticeship writing, reading, discovering his own clear voice. Many poems recall a happy childhood cut short by the early death of his mother, the poet Frances Horovitz. Many grieve for the loss of a recent love. Some move far from his childhood valley into mythology or another country, as in the striking, 'On the Broken Road'. Always, he gives the reader the very taste, colour, detail of a house, a kitchen, the valley, the sounds of a garden through an open door. Even in poems of loss there are flashes of joy: "A shivering flute-memory/ in the green of spring." At the heart of the collection is 'The Great Unlearning', a moving long poem for his father, unreeling their loving, troubled relationship backwards to the moment of his birth. I welcome this passionate collection, the first of many, I hope.'

From a review by *Anthony Rudolf* of *Next Year in Jerusalem* (2004) in the *Jewish Quarterly, Issue 195:*

'Tactful and tactile, [Adam Horovitz] has his own true voice, speaking his occasionally disturbing material with a light yet firm touch.'